# YOU ARE RICH

# YOU ARE RICH

By Passion Wade

*So You Can Write Publications, LLC*
*PO Box 80736*
*Milwaukee, WI 53208*
*www.sycwp.com*



*Publishing date: 5/3/2022*
*ISBN-13: 978-1-7376084-5-5*

*Cover design by: www.sycwp.com*
*Printed in the United States of America*

*(Note: "The majority of quotations gathered by the author have been frequently in print and/or movie and television, as well as publicly accessible on the Internet; considered public domain. Where possible, the author and publisher have made their best efforts to credit any available sources for them. In the cases where it was uncertain where they first appeared, the information was cited as "unknown" or "anonymous." The information in this book is intended to uplift and inspire all who read it, or who have it read to them. The information quoted was kept as it was found and/or heard by the author, who makes no guarantee that the information one-hundred percent accurate, just that the author intended for it to be beneficial to all who reads it, or has it read to them."*

SO YOU CAN WRITE PUBLICATIONS®

# ***Dedication(s)***

My mother, my grandparents, and my boy Fatz.

*- Passion Wade -*

# *Table of contents*

# *Introduction*

Rich - possessing or controlling great wealth.

Wealth - abundance of possessions or resources.

You are rich!

You may be wondering, "How am I rich?"

Well, for one, being rich is not physical, it is a state of mind. To be rich or to get rich you must possess certain characteristics and a certain type of mindset. To be rich financially, you must be rich mentally and spiritually.

The definition of rich is possessing or controlling great wealth, and the definition of wealth is abundance of possessions or resources. If you possess and control your mind which is abundant in knowledge, positive thoughts, determination, faith, motivation, and desire, then use those resources to help you create opportunity, you are already rich in mind and spirit. This means you have the ability to be rich financially. Always keep in mind that to be rich financially you must first be rich mentally and spiritually, and remember that you are rich! We all are. We just have to take control of our mind, use and develop our resources to create opportunities. That's what you will learn how to do in this book. Not only that, you will also learn how to generate active and passive income, and how to create positive cash flow. You will learn how the rich grow richer and how they manage their wealth by using an income statement and a balance sheet. You will learn the basics of Real Estate investing and how to protect your wealth; but most importantly, you will learn that you are rich!

Thank you.

# *PART ONE:*

# Rich in mind and spirit.

*"...I came to realize that poverty is not what's in your pocket, it's what you have in your head..."*

-John Bryant -

# Chapter (1)

## *Mindset: The power of dreaming big*

Mindset - An inclination or a fixed way of thinking.

The mindset is the most important factor in determining if a person will be poor, average, or wealthy. The mindset is often overlooked because it cannot be perceived with the five senses. In other words, it is intangible. You cannot see oxygen but it is vital to your body. In the same way, the right mindset is vital to your prosperity. You must believe in yourself, believe in your ability to create opportunities, be resilient and bounce back after taking a loss. You also have to be relentless in the pursuit of wealth. Let nothing stop you no matter what!

After years of researching and studying the mindsets of the world's richest people, we have discovered that every wealthy person on this earth or to ever walked the face of this earth (except those who've won the lottery or inherited wealth) has the same type of mindset which consists of these characteristics:

- Motivation -
- Think big/ have big goals -
- Strong desire to succeed -

It is critical that you develop every one of these traits. If you do not, you may as not even pursue wealth until you do. Let me explain why.

# - Motivation -

Motivation - A factor or circumstance that induces a person to act in a particular way.

What's driving you? If you have not thought about it, you should. Every person has different motivations but all motivations are not created equal. A good motivation should be driven with emotion and engrained into your belief system. For example, a person who wants to be wealthy so they can have fun might not work as hard as a person who wants to be wealthy so their kids do not have to grow up in poverty.

PERSON #1

| | | |
|---|---|---|
| | I want to have fun so I can be happy. | I want to get wealthy so I can have all the fun I want which in turn will make me happy. |
| Core Belief | Emotion | Motivation |

PERSON #2

| | | |
|---|---|---|
| If you love your children you won't let them grow up in poverty. | I don't want my children growing up in poverty because I love them. | I want to become wealthy so my children won't grow up in poverty. |
| Core Belief | Emotion | Motivation |

As you can see, although person #1's motivation is driven with emotion. There is no strong core belief to secure the emotions. If you are wondering why connecting your motivation with a strong core belief is important, let me tell you why. Emotions changed all of the time, how you feel today may not be how you feel tomorrow. Core beliefs on the other hand cannot be changed overnight. These are things that have been instilled in us throughout our lives.

Our own ideas developed from our personal experiences or programmed in us by our parents or close friends. Either way, once you have a strong core belief, to change it world equate to changing your entire personality. This is why selecting a motivation that aligns with a strong core belief is such an effective tool. It is not subject to change or bending, such as emotions are. Okay. Now, that we have an understanding to this concept, let's move on to the second attribute of a successful personality.

## - Thinking big/Having big goals -

Big - large in size, amount, or scope.

Goal - The object of a person's ambition or effort; a destination; an aim.

Having goal gives you a sense of direction, meaning, and purpose. If you want to be rich those goals must be big! What do you think long-term small goals are going to get you? Long-term small results and small success. If you have long-term big goals, you're going to achieve long-term big results and big success.

To achieve those big goals, you will have to break down those goals into smaller short-term goals that will eventually lead to accomplishing those big long-term goals.

Now, if you have small long-term goals you're going to have to have even smaller goals to accomplish those small long-term goal. By doing this, you are selling yourself short. There is nothing wrong we having small long-term goals, but if you want to be rich financially than you have yourself a problem. This is the difference in the mindsets of poor people, middle-class people, and rich people. There is even a difference and the mindset of millionaires and billionaire.

The different lies in how big or small the person thinks, or how big or small the thing or goal that the person is striving or aiming for. So, don't be afraid to aim for bigger goals.

*"...They said your dreams too big, now take a look at what I did..."*

- The Kid Laroi -

People will criticize you and tell you that your dreams are too big or unrealistic. Forget what they think. People will put their own limitations on you. Don't ever let anyone tell you what you can or cannot accomplish. Only you can determine that. Many people told me my dreams were unrealistic or too big, and as a result of me having those "big goals" and those "unrealistic dreams." I have accomplished in four years' time span - while incarcerated in prison -

more things than they had ever or will ever accomplish in their whole lifetime.

I have overcome poverty, became rich, I've written four books, started a company, created a clothing line, networked with successful and rich people, overcame depression, low self-esteem and a drug addiction. I have found internal joy and peace, became physically fit, discovered my purpose and inspired many people in prison to strive and chase after their dreams. This is the result of dreaming big and thinking big. The same things people told me were "unrealistic" or "too big" are the same things that propelled me to excel past them.

*"...Rich people think big, poor people think small..."*

- T. Harv Eker -

## - Strong desire to succeed -

Desire - An unsatisfied longing or craving.

Succeed - Accomplish, one's purpose.

A person with a strong desire to succeed will allow no one to stop him. He will do whatever it takes to get where he wants to be in life. Along with a strong desire to succeed comes determination.

Determination - Firmness of purpose.

Determination is key. I cannot overstate the importance of having determination while pursuing wealth. It doesn't matter who you are, or how well thought-out your plans and investment strategies are. We all reach a point in our journey when things become difficult. Adversity comes in many forms and although the market you are in maybe great, an issue in your personal life could make you ponder putting your journey on hold until the "right time." That's just it, there will never be a right time.

You have to navigate all obstacles with optimism, confidence, and determination. Let's say for example, you are a real estate investor, you may not want to get up and go check on your rental property, or crunch numbers for a great investment you heard about. If you allow these lapses in your determination, you will inevitably miss great opportunities or fail to correct small problems that can balloon into major problems. Determination propels one to commit.

Anyone with a strong desire to succeed will also exhibit perseverance.

Perseverance - Continue steadfastly or determinedly.

It is a simple, yet effective concept. It means to keep going when things are hard, to get up every time you fell down and refused to give up no matter what happens. Being able to persevere is critical to your success because like we said earlier, there will be hard times. There will be times when you want to give up, and if you give up you will never get to where you want to be. You must keep going after the setbacks. You may need to analyze yourself and your mistakes and learn from them. You also may need to seek council.

R.U. Darby stopped three-feet from gold.

A man named Darby who was digging to find gold. He borrowed money from his family to buy mining equipment. Once he bought the mining equipment he got to work without investing in the knowledge of how to mine which was detrimental to his success. After many weeks of rigorous work, he finally decides to give up and sold his mining equipment to a local junkman for $200. The junkman had done research on how to mine; he invested in knowledge.

He went in the mine and started digging where Derby had stopped and found a large Goldmine worth millions of dollars just three-feet away from where Darby had given up and stopped digging. This is a true story. You never know how close you are to success so never give up. You might be only three-feet away from your big payday.

# Chapter (2)

## *Education, Wisdom, and Knowledge*

Education - The act or process of educating or being educated.

There seems to be some confusion about the difference between education, wisdom, and knowledge.

Although they are similar, I will show you how they differ. When you go to school, you gain an education. You can get rich without a formal education. There are many multimillionaires that have not completed high school or gone to college. Now, we personally believe that having an institutional education is important for other aspects of life, but is not necessarily required to become wealthy. Another misconception that most people have is assuming that if they do get an education that they will automatically become wealthy.

We are sorry to inform you that many people with PhD's and Master's degrees work 9 to 5 jobs and live paycheck to paycheck.

Wisdom - Experience and knowledge together with the power of applying them critically or practically.

When you apply what you've learned and experience it you gain wisdom. You do not have to be wise to become rich. Many foolish people are rich. A lot of people in the entertainment business are very rich but are not wise whatsoever. To stay rich, you will surely need to be wise. Many people get rich and then end up broke. They do not have the wisdom or ability to manage the pressure, the problems, and the added responsibilities that comes with the success and wealth. It is harder to stay rich than it is to get rich. No matter how much money you make, you should continuously "educate" yourself and continuously apply what you learn every day for the rest of your life.

[ When I say educate yourself I mean by learning from your mistakes and by gaining and seeking knowledge.]

Knowledge - Specific information; facts or intelligence about something.

It's almost impossible to get rich without knowledge. Knowledge can be generalized (commonsense) or specialized (expert). To become rich, you will need both but especially specialized knowledge. Knowledge about a certain subject that exceeds the basic knowledge that the average person has is considered specialized knowledge. For example: my car breakdown and I know it is broke, this is general knowledge.

If you know how to fix the car means you have specialized knowledge because the average person doesn't know how to fix a car. You must apply this concept to whatever business or service you offer. Capitalize on your specialized knowledge of a subject by charging people for the use of that knowledge or use the knowledge yourself. What I mean by this is, when you charge somebody for the use of specialized knowledge, you are essentially being a paid consultant.

Continuing with the car example: charging someone to determine what is wrong with their car is charging for the use of specialized knowledge. On the other hand, if you were to fix the car for them you would be using the specialized knowledge yourself and make a larger profit. Or you could separate your time from money and create passive income (more on passive income in the second part of this book) by hiring someone with specialized knowledge and knows how to fix cars.

You pay them to do the dirty work while giving you more free time to spend with family and focus on other ways to make more money. If you do not have specialized knowledge on any subject, it should be your first priority to learn something others do not know because it will dramatically increase your earning potential. Capitalizing off of specialized knowledge is not the only aspect or reason why knowledge is required to get rich.

To get rich or to be successful in business, you must have the knowledge of how to get rich or how to be successful in business, or how to run a business or how to invest in real estate. Or whatever it is you want to do. People believe actors and musicians do not need knowledge because they are talented. This is false. In reality, many talented entertainers never make it because they lack knowledge on how the entertainment business works.

Without the knowledge of how to promote themselves and get paid for their skills, they're just another talented nobody. The principle is the same for businessman. You cannot run a successful business without understanding how a successful business operate. Did you know that 85% of all businesses fail?

I attribute that to all owners not knowing enough about their business.

Darby needed knowledge to.

Do you remember the story about how Darby, the only guy who was seeking to find gold? That was not just a story about perseverance, it was also a lesson on the power of knowledge. You see, Darby investing in the mining equipment, but not the knowledge of how to mine. The local junkman did. He received expert advice about mining and discovered that there was something call a fault line. This means that he would have to dig perpendicular from where Darby stopped digging and discovered gold just three feet away.

If Darby would have invested in the knowledge required to properly mine for gold, he would've found exactly what he was looking for without having to go through all of that unnecessary hard work. Yes, if he would have kept on going he could have saved himself time and energy. Moral of the story, both knowledge and perseverance are important.

More gold has been minded from the thoughts of men than has ever been taken from the earth.
-Napoleon Hill-

Set the highest standards.
- Evander Holyfield -

If people don't criticize you, then chances are you're probably not doing enough.
- Joe Donnelly -

It wasn't that their goals were too high or that they lacked ambition to succeed. It was that they allow others to set their limitations.
- Dr. Greg S. Reid -

Dream big and never stop short of reaching the top.
- Truett Cathy -

The most common cause of failure is quitting.
- Dr. Greg S. Reid -

# Worksheet

- Are you rich in mind and spirit? ___________

  If you answered no, then you must take control of your mind, your thoughts and develop the required characteristics and use those resources to create opportunities. Only then will you realize that you are rich.

- Are you motivated to succeed? ____________

- It is your motivation laced with strong core belief? _______________________________

- Do you have a strong desire to succeed? ____

- Are you're willing to go after your dreams with everything you got? ________________

- Are you willing to persevere and keep going no matter how hard times get? ____________

- Are you afraid to dream big? _____________

- Do you have big goals? __________________

# Chapter (3)

## *Writing down your goals*

Goal - The object of a person's ambition or effort; A destination; An aim.

Having a goal gives you a sense of direction, meaning, and purpose. Writing your goals down helps you visualize your dreams, rather than just a bunch of loose thoughts floating around in your head about the things you would like to see happen. A list of written goals can serve as a reminder of why you are hustling and what you are striving for. When you write your goals down, you take that first action step toward turning your dreams into reality.

Writing down long-term goals, mid-term goals, short-term goals, and short-short-term goals gives you a road map for your path to success with each completed goal being a milestone on that map. As soon as you are done reading this book, you should write down your goals. In the back of this book is goal sheets where you can write down your goals. Starting with your long-term goals, those things that you want to accomplish within 20 years from now.

Next, write down your mid-term goals, those goals which you would like to reach within 10 years. Then, put your short-term goals, those which what you want to accomplish within 5 years. And finally, your short-short-term goals, the things you would like to carry out within a year. The shorter-term goals should lead into and help accomplish the longer-term goals.

Here is an example: (Be specific when writing your goals down)

*** Long-term Goals (20 years)**

- To have a net worth of $10 billion or more.
- My company "Royalty Investors" will be a fortune 500 company with $5 billion in annual revenue.
- To own over $100 million dollars' worth of real estate.
- To have started a nonprofit organization that provide housing and resources for homeless people.

*** Mid-term Goals (10 years)**

- To have a net-worth of $100 million dollars.
- My company "Royalty Investors" will be on its way to being a fortune 500 company with over $50 million dollars in annual revenue.
- To own over $20 million dollars' worth of real estate.

*** Short-term Goals (5 years)**

- To have a net-worth of $10 million dollars.
- My company will be getting off the ground and finally profitable.
- I will own at least 5 rental properties.

*** Short-short-term Goals (1 year)**

- To have completed an online business class.
- To have read 3 rental properties books, 3 self-help books, and 3 business books.
- To have done a lot of research about owning and running a successful business.

Your goals will be different from those listed above, this is just an example. Your goals may not be as big as them and that's okay, but don't sell yourself short. Your goals may even be big bigger than the goals listed above and that's okay, but make sure they are goals you will truly commit to. Also, you should write down daily goals but don't overwhelm yourself. I have done this, I used to write down too many daily goals and could never commit to them because there is only so much you can do in one day. So, when writing your daily goals list, keep it to about two or three things, and get into the habit of always completing them. Here is an example:

* Monday Goal

- Read first chapter of "Think and Grow Rich."
- Write down business plan.
- Watch a motivational video on YouTube.

# Chapter (4)

## *Planning*

Plan - A formulated and especially detailed method by which a thing is to be done.

Planning is also very important. There is a saying that goes, "If you fail to plan, then you plan to fail." You must plan out every detail of the situation if you want to be successful. Do not leave anything to chance and control the whole process. Never go into a money-making situation without a plan of action. Your plans should be specific, realistic, and in line with your overall goal. Planning takes the pressure off of you when it is time to make tough decisions because you already know what you are going to do. This makes for less confusion and therefore fewer costly mistakes are made.

[Note: In the back of this book there is a plan worksheet which gives you the opportunity to write down what your plan is.]

A dream is just a dream until it is written down. Only then it does it become a goal.
- Jonathan Buckland -

A goal is a contract with yourself and should be based less on what you want to do and more on what you promise yourself you'll actually accomplish.
- Jonathan Buckland -

Dreams without education, plans, mentors, and actions create delusional people.
- Donald Trump -

Let your major goal be automatic pilot. When your goal absorbs you, you'll find yourself making the right decisions to reach your goals.
- David Schwartz -

The most intelligent man living cannot succeed in accumulating money - nor in any other undertaking without plans which are practical and workable.
- Napoleon Hill -

# *PART TWO:*

# Rich in Finances

*"...Being a cashflow millionaire allows me to pay less and taxes, legally, without selling assets which would decrease my net-worth. And allow me to use that as money..."*

- Robert Kiyosaki -

# Chapter (5)

## *Assets and liabilities*

Asset - Anything that produces income or appreciates, and has a ready market.

Liability - An expense that takes money out of your pocket.

**Assets can be:**

- Royalties from intellectual property such as scripts and patents.
- Royalties from books, music or business investments.
- Paper assets such as stocks and bonds.
- Notes (IOUS)
- Business income.
- Income from rental properties.
- And anything that produces passive income.

(More on passive income in the next chapter)

**Liabilities can be:**

- Mortgage payment.
- Car note.
- Non-producing income investments.
- Consumer debt.
- And anything else that does the opposite of producing passive income.

Most people wrongly believe that all of the big-ticket items that they purchase our assets. They think that their jewelry, cars and primary residences are assets. The bank or other financial advisors may tell you that your home is an asset but that is false. Remember, an asset is something that puts money in your pocket or produces income. Never listen to financial advisors if they are broke or do not own any real assets themselves.

More about this in a later chapter. The reason why people are in debt is because they spend their earned income on liabilities instead of assets. Think about it. All the poor people you know either has a car note, a mortgage payment, college debt, credit card debt, etc.... but don't own any real assets. That's why they are poor. They do not invest in their asset column.

This is what their balance sheet looks like:

| Assets | Liabilities |
| --- | --- |
| * None | * Car note<br>* Mortgage<br>* Credit card debt<br>* College debt |

Here's what a wealthy person's balance sheet looks like:

| Assets | Liabilities |
| --- | --- |
| * Royalties<br>* Stocks<br>* Business income<br>* Real Estate | * Investment debt |

Your house is not asset.
- Robert Kiyosaki -

The rich buy assets, the poor only have expenses, the middle class by liabilities they think are assets.
- Robert Kiyosaki -

An asset puts money in my pocket, a liability takes money out of your pocket.
- Robert Kiyosaki -

If you want to be rich, simply spend your life buying or building assets. If you want to be poor or middle-class, spend your life buying liabilities.
- Robert Kiyosaki -

You want the asset not you producing income.
- Author of the Wall Street Money Machine -

# Chapter (6)

## *Acquire multiple streams of income*

To build wealth by creating positive cashflow you must learn how to acquire multiple streams of income and to do that you must understand all the different types of income there is and which ones will best serve you.

### Different types of income

* Earned income - Earned income is your primary income stream through a job. For most, earned income is very limiting and has attracted the acronym "Just Over Broke." In other words, you earn this just enough to survive.

* Active income - Your business is most likely using an active income stream, this is where are you do some work or provide a service and someone pays you for it. Very simple and a direct connection between the work and payment.

* Passive income - Passive income is where the income is not directly tied to the work you do. The work needed for a passive income stream takes place early on and the income flows in passively later. Let's say you buy a single home rental property, the property may have to first be worked on and fixed up, then you will have to find a tenant and he or she pays you the required monthly rent that the income becomes passive. In my own personal opinion, I believe that this is the best income to acquire because it gives you the

opportunity to separate your time from money, which means you make money while spending your time doing something else like traveling the world or using your time to create more passive income. And or create other types of income all at the same time. Unlike earned income, because once you stop working your income stops. You also can't acquire as many streams of passive income as you like.

* Profit income - By selling a service or products for more than they cost you is the basis of profit income. Profit income can be a stream of passive income also, if you hire people to sell the service or products for you. Active income can be a passive stream of income if you hire people to run a business for you.

* Interest income - If you or your business has spare cash sitting in a bank account it is losing money. Instead, you could put your money to work by investing in a savings scheme and use the power of compound interest to gain a passive income. Buying government bonds is an investment that will generate interest.

* Royalty income - This is a passive income stream generated by designing, or making something and charging people and businesses for it. Musicians are a prime example, for every album sold and every time it is played to the public, they receive a royalty payment. Another example of royalty income is when an author gets a book published and sells it through their publisher he/she receives a royalty payment for every book sold. Or say an investor wants to invest in your company, instead of him wanting equity (a percentage of the profits from your business) he may ask for a

royalty, a certain amount of money per unit (products or service) sold. Thee investor receives royalty income.

* Portfolio income - Is income derived from paper assets such as stocks and bonds. This also can be considered passive income.

* Rental income - Property investments are an excellent way of protecting your money and generating passive income from rent.

Now that you know and understand all the different types of income, it is important that you understand the relationship between an income statement and a balance sheet. An **income statement** is what you used to keep track of how much income you have flowing in and how much of that income you are spending on expenses. Here is what an income statement looks like:

| Income | Expenses |
|---|---|
| * 5,000 a month from rental properties | * 2,000 a month on food and supplements |

Income Statement

A **balance sheet** is used to keep track of your income producing investments and your debt. Here is what a balance sheet looks like:

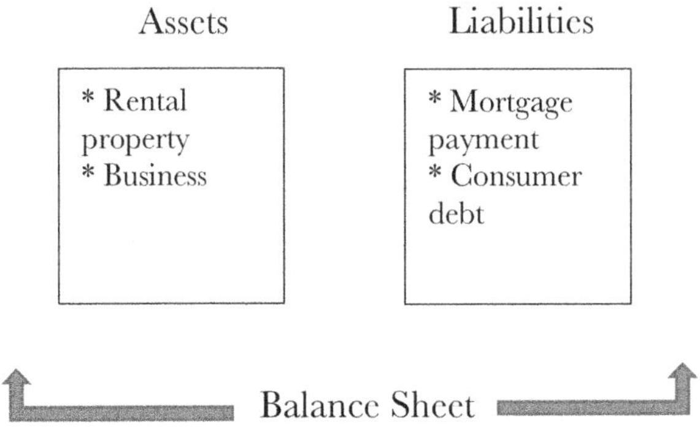


Remember, that your assets and liabilities are your balance sheet, and your income and expenses are your income statement. To get rich and stay rich you must keep track of where every dollar is going. Using the balance sheet and income statement to build wealth is essential. Remember when I said you must acquire multiple streams of income? Well, what that really means is acquire as many assets as possible. The assets are what produce the income. The bottom line to wealth is duplication and repetition.

You want to duplicate your income and repeat that process over and over. But you can't do this with all incomes and all and incomes aren't considered assets, like earned income. Earned income is income you have to work for and is earned on an hourly basis. You cannot acquire money of this type of income because there are only so many hours in a day that your body can physically work. Earned income is not an asset because it takes away from your free time and your potential to create many streams of passive income.

Most of you may have to start out with earned income and may be drowning in debt. Well, don't worry because you can use the income statement and the balance sheet to help you get out of debt and transition from making earned income to making passive income. You must first start off by creating a positive cashflow. And to do that you may have to cut back on expenses because you made more money flowing in their money flowing out.

Let's say you make $10,000 a year and you're spending $12,000 (using credit, getting loans or starting down payments you know you will have to pay back plus interest; consumer debt) a year. You are creating a negative cashflow. You are growing broker every year and putting yourself $2,000 deeper in debt every year. Here's is what your income statement and balance sheet look like:

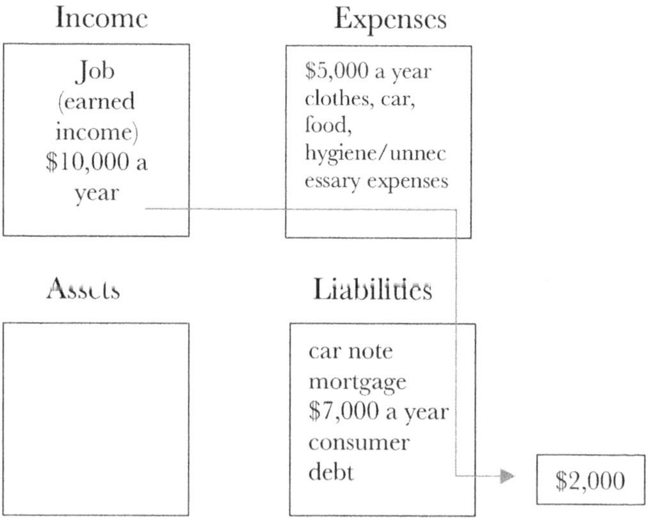

But let's say you may $10,000 dollars a year but you only spend $8,000 a year on expenses and liabilities. You have created a positive cashflow and you're growing $2,000 richer every year. Here's what your income statement and balance sheet will looked like:

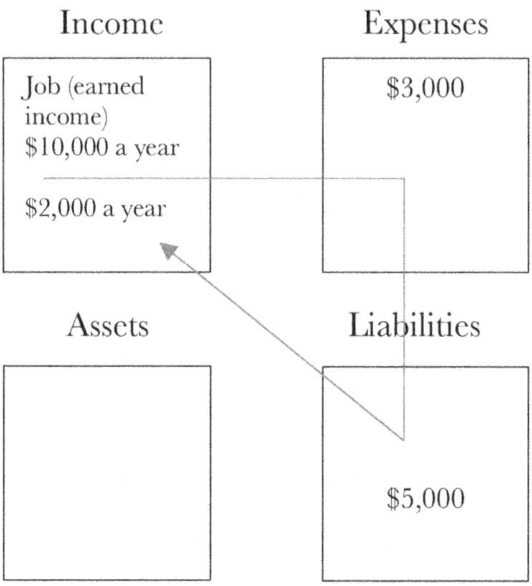


This is a good start but to transition from making earned income to making passive income you must start investing in your asset column. Make investing in your asset column a priority. You must pay yourself first. Your asset column is more important than your expenses and liability column because your asset column will take care of all your other columns. [Liabilities, expenses, and income]. This is what your income statement and balance sheet would look like before your asset column starts generating nice amounts of income and you decrease your expenses:

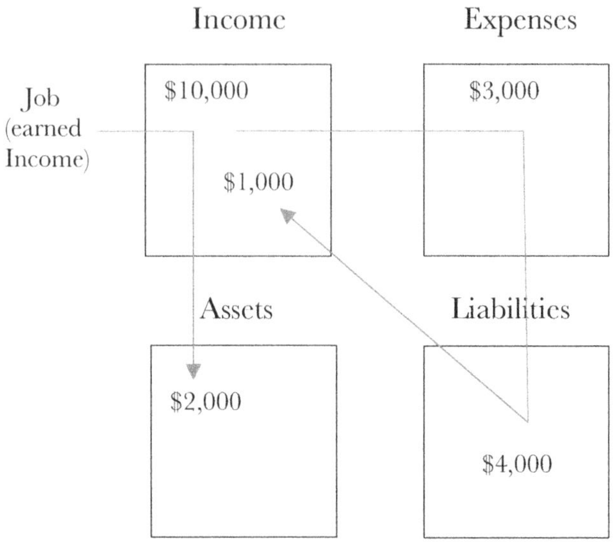


I don't believe in living below your means but if you want to build wealth and eventually be able to enjoy luxuries all while still growing richer, you will have to make some sacrifices to get there. You're going to have to cut back on your expenses. Once you are rich and generating large amounts of passive income you can enjoy those luxuries you've always dreamed of having as long as it doesn't put you in a negative cashflow deficit.

In my personal opinion, I don't believe there is anything wrong with owning a Ferrari and a mansion if you can afford it, why not? Some may say, "Why waste so much money on a house and a car when you can use that money to give back?" Well, for one, if you are an entrepreneur and you own a business and or real estate, or you invest in companies or write educational books, you are giving back! How so? Well, you are providing jobs, housing, and most importantly education, knowledge, and resources and opportunities for the community.

Personally, I invest am in non-profit organizations and charities. I have created and are developing my own non-profit organization, and my business alone provide resources, education, knowledge and opportunities for others. So, to those who give back and provide resources and opportunities for others have a right to enjoy their hard-earned wealth, because in reality, no one is entitled or required by law to help anyone else but themselves.

Although, I do not agree that it is the right thing to do, but I also believe that we should reward ourselves for our effort. Back to what I was saying about transitioning from making earned income to making passive income. Here is what your income statement and balance sheet would look like after your asset column starts producing large amounts of income and you pay off all your consumer debt:

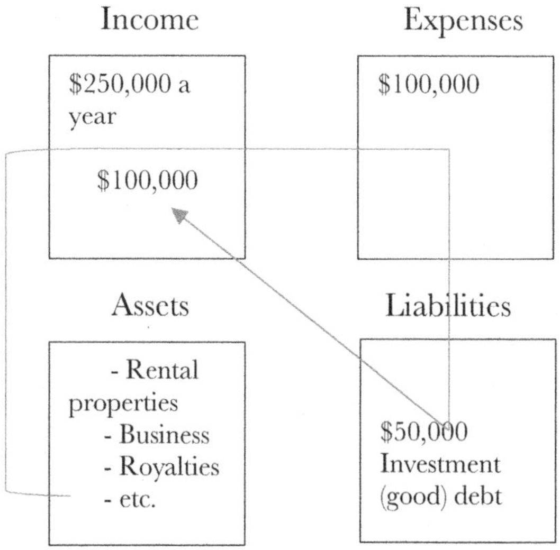

As long as continue to build your asset column, your annual (yearly) income will always grow. Soon you will have millions of dollars in passive income flowing in.

Buying or building assets that deliver cash flow is putting your money to work for you.
- Robert Kiyosaki -

Separated your time from money.
- Alex Becker -

All rich entrepreneurs have at least seven streams of income flowing in.
- Anonymous -

Each dollar in my asset column was a great employee, working hard to make more employees and buy the boss a new Porsche.
- Robert Kiyosaki -

The ability to become wealthy is the ability to convert earned income into passive income.
- Robert Kiyosaki -

# Worksheet

- Ankle you think will best serve you and why?

  ______________________________________
  ______________________________________
  ______________________________________
  ______________________________________

- Are you going to start investing in your asset column?

  ______________________________________

- Are you going to make investing in your asset column a priority? ____________________

- Are you going to convert your art income into passive income? And how will you do it?

  ______________________________________
  ______________________________________
  ______________________________________
  ______________________________________

- Write down your current assets. (If you own any)

- Write down your liabilities.

# Chapter (7)

## *Debt; Leverage*

Some people use debt and get poor.
Some people use debt and get rich.

How is that possible?

Well, it depends on why you're using the debt and what kind of debt you are using. Are you using debt to buy luxuries or something that you want but can't afford? Or are you using debt to pay for an investment because you don't have all the money for it, or simply because you don't want to use your money for it? In other words, are using debt to buy liabilities? Or are you using debt to buy assets? Are you using consumer debt or are you using investment debt?

### Leverage

To build wealth you must understand the term leverage and how to use it to build wealth. Leverage is learning how to do more with less. A professional investor may have $200,000 in his/her bank account and they find a good rental property that cost $100,000. What do you think they're going to do? If you guessed that they would take $100,000 out of their bank account and purchase the rental property, you are wrong! A professional investor would know that it would be wiser to use leverage to purchase a rental property. Why? Well, because leverage means doing more with less by using OPM or OPT.

OPM = Others people's money, management, or mind.
OPT = Other people's time or talents.

In this case we are talking about other people's money, (private money lenders, banks, investors, or credit) The professional investor knows that when investing in real estate that in most cases you only have to put 20% of the asking price down and you can use OPM to pay the other 80%. You may be wondering, why not just use your own money? When you use OPM, not only do you get to save money, but you get 100% of all the benefits by using only 20% your money. You receive 100% benefits appreciation, income, tax benefits and amortization (paying off investment debt suddenly) while the bank or other investors receive none of those benefits. Although they do get paid back their money plus interest, you receive all the benefits. Even if you don't have all the money for an investment, you can still use OPM. As long as you have at least 20% of the asking price. In some cases, may be required to pay a higher percentage of asking price or sometimes even lower. This doesn't just apply to real estate, you can also use OPM to invest in starting a business, buying a franchise or almost anything you invest in. There are other types of financial leverage, such as the leverage of financial intelligence, or other people's financial intelligence. Leverage is also anything that makes your job a little easier. It's easier to use OPT to help you build wealth and make sophisticated investment decision or to run your business.

Work your strengths, and hire your weakness.
- Anonymous -

Business owner uses leverage by using OPT, by hiring other people to work for them. Or by hiring people to do the things they don't know how to do. People get rich off debt because they understand and use leverage.

If you want to know more about building wealth using leverage, I recommend you read, "The 5 Financial IQ's" Robert Kiyosaki.

The beauty of using the banks money is that it's tax-free money.
- Robert Kiyosaki -

Learn to do more with less.
- Robert Kiyosaki -

# **Worksheet**

- Are you going to use consumer debt or are you going to use investment debt? And why?

____________________________________________
____________________________________________
____________________________________________
____________________________________________

- Are you going to use OPM and OPT to build wealth?

____________________________________________
____________________________________________
____________________________________________
____________________________________________

- And why?

____________________________________________
____________________________________________
____________________________________________
____________________________________________

# Chapter (8)

## *Protecting your wealth*

If you have started your journey and are building wealth, you must learn know how to protect your wealth.

To protect your wealth, you should learn more about corporations. A corporation is an entity that allows you to protect your wealth by separating your assets. It's kind of like you are creating a single life form for each asset.

Here's an example: A man we'll call "John" owns two properties. One title is held under his name, and the other title is held in the name of a corporation. Let's say a person falls on each of the properties due to negligence and pursues a judgement against John. The person whom fell on the property that is held under the name of the corporation, can only seek compensation from the assets held under the name of that particular corporation. While the person whom fell on the property held under John's name can go after anything that John owns.

Anytime you start a business or buy real estate, you can incorporate that asset. To learn more on corporations, I recommend you read, "Start Your Own Corporation" by Garret Sutton. And/or research more on corporations on the internet.

Before you incorporate anything, it is important that you have an attorney present because certain corporations work best for certain individuals and assets.

Another way to protect your wealth and your assets is to hire an accountant, financial advisor and in a business attorney.

It is important to know that not all financial advisors are the same. Before hiring an advisor, you should first make sure that they understand your vision and their actually practice what they preach. An advisor should not give you any advice about assets or real estate if they do not own any real assets or any real estate. And if you find a financial advisor you think is good and hire them, and they tell you anything that goes completely against your vision and your wealth, fire him/her instantly and find a new one.

# Chapter (9)

## *Basics of Real Estate Investing*

The reason we are teaching the basics but because real estate is arguable the best way to protect and build shorter wealth.

### Choosing a property type

Once you've decided that you want to become a real estate investor, you have to act, you have to get the ball rolling. To start you have to pick a community and a property type for your investments. Since you're just beginning, I suggest you start with residential properties in low income communities. This is a very strategic choice to make more money. There are multiple reasons for this choice such as saving money on purchasing price, saving money on repairs, guarantee government payment etc.

These are also great options because they are relatively small and easy to manage. They also don't require complex formulas to check if they will be profitable. With some basic math you should be able to determine if your investment will make you money. So, these are your options:

- Single family residence (1 unit)
- Multi-unit properties (2 to 4 units)
- Townhouses (4 or more units)

I personally believe that multi-unit properties are the best properties to start with because you can take advantage of a wonderful program offered by the FHA (Federal Housing Administration) for the first-time homeowners. The program allows you to purchase a property with a little money down. The down payment is usually between 0% and 3.5%. (you must live in one of the units to take advantage of this program as an investment).

This is a great savings because a down payment for a conventional mortgage can cost between 20% to 30% of the purchase price. That's extra money that could have been used for furnishing your property, making repairs or improvements. This isn't the only benefit though; you can jumpstart your real estate empire because buy living in one of the units and renting the other units out will allow you to live basically rent-free and you save money for your next venture. Here's an example:

Purchase price: $150,000

Multi-unit Property

| Unit #1 | Unit #2 | Unit #3 | Unit #4 |
|---|---|---|---|
| Rent<br>$1,000 | Rent<br>$1,000 | Your home | Rent<br>$1,000 |

Monthly Mortgage: $1,500
Total rent collected: $3,000
Profit: $1,500

As you can see, your monthly mortgage is $1,500 and your monthly income from this property is $3,000. That leaves you with $1,500 profit. That might not sound like much but compared to losing money every month paying rent to a landlord. You're essentially getting paid to live in your own place. Also, if you factor in equity build up (the percentage of the property paid off) this becomes a great deal. Not only have you created a passive income stream but you are passively paying of an asset (investment debt; Amortization).

## Repairs

You will likely need to make some repairs so tenants will actually want rent the apartment. There are actually different types of repairs so let me break them down for you:

- Safety repairs: These are the most important repairs. They must be done to make sure the property is safe to live in. Here are a few examples of safety repairs: removing mold, covering exposed wiring, replacing missing floor boards etc. Be sure to tend to all safety repairs because failure to do so could lead to someone being injured or killed on your properties.

- Beauty repairs: Are exactly what they sound like, repairs to increase the beauty of a property. Examples of beauty repairs would be repainting a bedroom or installing carpet. These repairs do not have to be done in order to rent the apartment out to a tenant, but doing them might enable you to increase the rental prices, thus earning more profit from your investment.

Another thing you must understand is the type of people they will be renting your properties. People whom will most likely be low income and have not experienced the finer things of life. There is a upside and downside to this so let me give you the bad news first:

Since people have not experience the finer things in life, it is likely that they don't know how to properly care for a home. So, expect more property damage and maybe some complaints from neighbors.

The Good news: Since most people haven't experienced the finer things in life, they're less likely to make a big deal about small repairs, which can add up and become quite costly. Another plus is that many people are on government assistance programs that help them pay their rent. This means a secure rental payment from the government to you, no chasing a tenant for payments.

# 1031 Exchange

The 1031 exchange rolls the gain from your old investment property over to your new investment property while allow you to delay paying income tax on that profit. The 1031 is the IRS code section that governs this rollover.

The 1031 exchange is a tool used by most advanced investors but over-looked by many smaller investors. Do not forget to take advantage of this opportunity to delay paying taxes on your profit, it could cost you thousands and slow the progression of building your real estate empire. The 1031 exchange allows you to delay paying the income taxes that you have to pay when you normally sell your property. If you sell a property within the first year of owning it, you will be taxed for it as "ordinary income" at 33%. Let's say you hold that same property for one year and then sell it, this sell will still be taxed, taxed as "long term capital gains" at 15%. Now if you hypothetically sell that property at any rate: using the 1031 tax deferred exchange, you will delay paying that tax until you sell your final property without using the 1031 exchange method.

The loophole is that you never have to sell a property out right and can delay paying that tax indefinitely. Let me explain the benefit of 1031 exchanges with a simple example:

### Scenario #1: Taxed as ordinary income

Make $100,000 profit which gets taxed ordinary income 33%.

Profit: $100,000 hundred thousand
Taxed: $33,000
Left for reinvestment: $67,000

You can take that $67,000 and put 10% down on a $670,000 house. Now you turn around and sell that house for $800,000, making a profit of $130,000. You get taxed 33% on that $130,000 as ordinary income.

Profit: $130,000
Taxed: $42,900
On this deal you get to keep: $87,100

You also get your original $67,000 back.

You have: $67,000 + $87,100 = $154,000 to invest. You've paid $75,900 in taxes between these two deals.

You can now put 10% down on a $1,540,000.

### Scenario #2: Taxed as 1031 deferred

Make $100,000 on real estate sale, not taxed as income because it's 1031 deferred.

Profit: $100,000
Taxed: 0
What you're left with: $100,000 for reinvestment.

You can't take that $100,000 and put 10% on a $1,000,000 house. Now you turn around and sell that house for $1,194,030 (~19.4% more than you bought it for, the same the other deal. 670k-800k is proportion to 1m-1.194m) Making a profit of $194,030. You delay paying taxes using the 1031 exchange method, and can't reinvest all of it. You also get your original $100,000 back. You have $294,030 to invest - you paid no taxes.

You can now put 10% down on a $2,940,00 house. See the difference?

By using the 1031 exchange method, you're able to take the money off one real estate deal and immediately invest in another one without being taxed like you would be if you just "cashed out" for each deal. In Scenario #1, the investor cashed out after each deal and was taxed at 33% on his income. The investor in Scenario #2, rolled his profits over into new real estate purchases and paid no taxes. Look at the difference, after only two deals, the investor is Scenario #2 has about $140,000 more purchasing power then investor in Scenario #1. That's a big difference. Bigger deals = bigger profits. If we suppose they sell their respective $1,540,000 and $2,940,000 houses for 19.4% more than they paid for them again: The investor in Scenario #1 will make a $298,760 profit, while the investor in Scenario #2 will make $570,360. It's easy to see that the second investor is on to something.

Disclaimer: Although the 1031 Exchange is a great tool, it also has certain stipulations so be sure to check with a legal advisor before jumping in head first!

# *PART THREE:*

# Rich in Mind & Spirit and Finances Workbook

*Completing this workbook gives you the opportunity to act and another step toward your financial freedom. It is also scientifically proven that when you think about and write things down you are more likely to remember and apply what you've learned.*

# Your Goals

## Long-Term Goals (20 years)

{Use this page to write out your goals}

# Mid-Term Goals (10 years)

{Use this page to write out your goals}

# Short-Term Goals (5 years)

{Use this page to write out your goals}

# Short-Short-Term Goals (1 year)

{Use this page to write out your goals}

# What is your plan?

{Use this page to write out your plan}

# What steps will you take today toward your dreams?

{Use this page to write out your steps}

# Statement of Desire

This is a worksheet/action plan used in "Think and Grow Rich." You write down the exact overall amount of money you desire, what will you do or give in return to reach that amount? And when do you plan to acquire the money by?

## What expenses can you cut back on that will allow you to save more money and create a positive cashflow?

# What does your income statement and balance sheet look like right now?

{Fill out the boxes}

**Income** **Expenses**

**Income Statement**

**Assets** **Liabilities**

**Balance Sheet**

# What do you want your income statement and balance sheet to look like? (20 years from now)

{Fill out the boxes}

**Income** **Expenses**

**Income Statement**

**Assets** **Expenses**

**Balance Sheet**

# Affirmations

Affirmations are used to increase your desire to succeed, to increase your faith that you will succeed, and to encourage and motivate you. (Therapist, Physiatrist, and AA instructors uses affirmations as a tool to help their clients be more positive and to help them succeed in their endeavors. Also, motivational speakers, philosophers and business man uses affirmations to motivate themselves to say determined to succeed.)

Below are some affirmations you should read every day, when you wake up or when you feel like giving up. Also, read them before bed and feel free to add some of your own.

- I will be successful
- I will succeed
- I will be rich
- I will be a multi-millionaire
- I am rich
- I am positive
- I am determined to succeed
- I will persevere
- I am a business man/woman

Write some of your own: ____________________

____________________

____________________

____________________

____________________

____________________

____________________

____________________

____________________

____________________

____________________

Read both lists every day.

# Why do you want to be rich? What's driving/motivating you?

From the "Secret of the Millionaire Mind Quotes" we present you with the 17 Wealth files. (Keep in mind that we're talking about mentally, spiritually, and financially rich people.)

1. Rich people believe "I create my life"
Poor people believe "Life happens to me"

2. Rich people play the money game to win
Poor people play the money game not to lose

3. Rich people are committed to being rich
Poor people want to be rich

4. Rich people think big
Poor people think small

5. Rich people focus on opportunities
Poor people focus on obstacles

6. Rich people admire other rich and successful
Poor resent rich and successful people

7. Rich people associate with positive successful people
Poor people associate with negative unsuccessful people

8. Rich people are willing to promote themselves and their value
Poor people think negative about selling and promoting

9. Rich people are bigger than their problems
Poor people are smaller than their problems

10. Rich people are excellent receivers
Poor people are poor receivers

11. Rich people choose to get paid based on results
Poor people get paid based on time

12. Rich people think both
Poor people think "either/or"

13. Rich people focus on their net worth
Poor people focus on their working income

14. Rich people manage money well
Poor people mismanage money well

15. Rich people have their money work hard for them
Poor people work hard for their money

16. Rich people act in spite of fear
Poor people let fear stop them

17. Rich people constantly learn and grow
Poor people are ignorant

## What do you think these means? Do you think like poor people or rich people?

To be rich you must know the difference between thee mindset of the rich and the mindset of the poor. [Start thinking like the rich]

| The mindset of the rich<br>———————<br>Wealthy People…. | The mindset of the poor<br>———————<br>Poor People…. |
|---|---|
| * Have self-discipline | * Lack self-discipline |
| * Understands how money works | * Doesn't understand how money works |
| * Isn't afraid to take risks | * Afraid to take risks |
| * Create passive income | * Live off earned income |
| * Are financially literate | * Ignorant when it comes to money |
| * Acquire assets | * Acquire liabilities |
| * Buys luxuries last | * Buys luxuries first |
| * Focus on their asset column | * Focus on expenses/liabilities |
| * Understands financial statements/investment strategies | * Have no ideal financial statements exist/ or what they're for |
| * Choose friends wisely | * Hangs around unsuccessful/negative people |
| * Keeps their insights on winning | * Keeps their insights on the things they want right now |
| * Uses assets to buy luxuries | * Uses earned income to buy luxuries that are liabilities |

# Quotes from successful, rich entrepreneurs:

Dreams are wonderful things and allow us to see the big picture; goals are simply dreaming with deadlines.
- Author of Networking in the music Business -

You either do it or you don't, trying doesn't count.
- Author of Networking in the music Business -

Money problems make you smarter… if you solve the problem. If you solve your money problem, your financial intelligence grows, you become richer. If you do not solve your money problem you become poorer. If you do not solve your money problem, that problem often grows into ore problems.
- Robert Kiyosaki -

The key to becoming rich is to recognize that the system is unfair, learn the rules and use them to your advantage.
- Robert Kiyosaki –

What do you think those quotes mean and why?

A journey of a thousand miles starts with a single step.
- Lao TZU -

The Chief cause of failure and unhappiness is trading what you want most for what you want now.
- Zack Ziglar -

One of the main weakness is the average man's familiarity with the word "Impossible." He knows all the rules which will not work, he knows all the things which cannot be done.
- Napoleon Hill -

Success comes to those who become success conscious.
- Napoleon Hill –

Wishing will not bring wishes, but desiring wishes with a state of mind becomes an obsession, then plannin definite ways and means to acquire riches and backing those plans with persistence which does not recognize failure, will bring riches.
- Napoleon Hill -

What do you think those quotes mean and why?

_______________________________________________

_______________________________________________

_______________________________________________

_______________________________________________

_______________________________________________

_______________________________________________

_______________________________________________

_______________________________________________

_______________________________________________

# Afternote

Apply what you learned and you will be successful. And only, if you truly apply these principles in his book and refuse to give up then can I guarantee that you will be rich financially.

I have overcome property and became rich mentally. So, I know that these principles work, and is the reason why I wanted to share these principles with the world.

I am grateful and honored to have the ability to share this information with you.

May wealth, abundance, success, prosperity be with you.

# Acknowledgements

I would like to acknowledge everyone who has doubted me in my life. Thank you for inspiring me to defy the odds and become everything you said I couldn't be. Shout out to: Jerog Fowler, Cameona Kelly, Matthew Conant, Desmond Lindsey, and everyone who are trying to build a better life for themselves.

*- Passion Wade -*

# Recommended Reads

- "Think and Grow Rich" By Napoleon Hill
- "Rich Dad Poor Dad" By Robert Kiyosaki
- "Secrets of the Millionaire Mind" By T. Harv Eker
- "10 Pillars of wealth" By Alex Becker
- "7 Habits of Highly Effective People" By Stephen R. Covey
- "7 Habits of Highly Effective Prisoner" By Randy L. Fosterling
- "Start Your Own Corporation" By Garret Sutton
- "Loopholes of Real Estate" By Garret Sutton

# Credits

Definitions - The Merriam Webster dictionary

Resources and Data - Robert Kiyosaki; "Rich Dads Increase your Financial IQ"

Recourses and Data - Napoleon Hill; "Think and Grow Rich"

Recourses and Data - T. Harv Eker; "Secrets of the Millionaire Mind"

SO YOU CAN WRITE
PUBLICATIONS®

"Where the writers go…"
www.sycwp.com

Made in the USA
Monee, IL
04 November 2026

67378944R00049